CONTENTS

A DEVELOPMENTAL ANALYSIS OF PRE-COLONIAL AFRICAN ECONOMY

RAJI AFEEZ TOPE

FOREWORD

◆ ◆ ◆

Development is a porous concept. It is often relative in outlook and usually has no generally accepted yardstick. Consequently, the relativity of the term has been largely manipulated by European Colonizers in their wholesale designation of pre-colonial African economy as underdeveloped. Through the qualitative mode of historical analysis, this study probes into the nature and structure of pre-colonial African economy. It is found that far from being underdeveloped, it was self-sustaining and continuously expanding, save the perceived obstacles. The obstacles were taken into consideration in subsequent analysis. This piece concludes that, due to the self-sustaining feature of this economy, it may be said to be relatively developed. Therefore, any attempt to describe it otherwise is either a form of double standard proportion or description hypocrisy.

RAJI Afeez Tope

Raftmedia Outreach

Ofatedo (Osogbo) Nigeria

26/10/2019

INTRODUCTION

◆ ◆ ◆

The economy is integral to culture. Even if human beings do not live by bread alone, the search for bread in Africa takes an eternity. As in the Stone Age human beings spent almost all their time seeking food, the struggle to survive consumes the majority of the population.[1] The structure of pre-colonial African economy was chiefly agricultural, non-agricultural ventures and exchange and marketing system.[2] Though its sophisticated development is admitted in some quarters while some, especially the Eurocentric writers and their African supporters supposes no benefit existed in African pre-colonial economy. This assertion of theirs might have been informed by the fact that pre-colonial African economy as "sophisticated" as it is was bedeviled by a number of obstacles, an analysis of which shall constitute a thrust of this discourse.

Awolowo once remarked that the problems which beset our ancestors from the beginning of the Stone Age up to the eve of Africa's contact with the white race were - ignorance, technical backwardness, superstitious beliefs, poverty, diseases, primitive cultivation of land, poor maintenance and so on.[3] while his claim about this might be viewed as containing some element of truth, it need be stressed that despite these obstacles which severally ravaged pre-colonial African economy, Africans still managed to survive relatively. Of course his claims was not because Africans were socio-economically feeble in my own estimation but based such supposition on a comparism with the 'white standard', which should not necessarily thrive, given the fact that these (Africa and Europe) are separate entities which did not develop at the same pace altogether, under the same environmental impulse and psychological dictates, hence the possibility of evolving different socio-economic, developmental outlook.

THE CONCEPT OF ECONOMIC DEVELOPMENT

◆ ◆ ◆

Development is a complex issue, with many different and sometimes contentious definitions. There is no single index of measuring development, as such it has placed it conceptualization on a zigzag mode. A succinct understanding of the concept can however be built around scholastic perception on the theme.

A basic perception equates development with economic growth.[4] this is perhaps what Rodney implies when he avers about development; 'development implies an increasing capacity to regulate internal and external relationships.[5]he furthers that development was universal because the conditions leading to economic expansion were universal. This has a dual implication; that the concept of development is not a sectoral monopoly as per certain climes of the world and that such conditions leading to development is an aggregate of a complex process of intra and inter-state relationships.

On the specifics, economic development usually refers to the adoption of new technologies, transition from agriculture-based to industrial-based economy, and general improvement in living standard.[6] literally, economic development can be defined as "passage from lower to higher stage which implies change"[7] It is perhaps in the same vein that Herrick suppose; economic development is generally defined as to include improvement in material welfare especially for persons with the lowest incomes, eradication of mass poverty with its correlates of illiteracy, disease and early death, changes in composition of imputes and outputs that generally include shifts in the underlying structure of production away from agriculture towards industrial activities.[8] as inferred from these conceptual perceptions the dominant themes dictating economic development is changes, shifts, adaptations, and receptions in the prime factors of the economy. An assessment of how these played out in the pre-colonial African economy shall herein be discussed. What is however clear is that the pre-colonial African economy is not stagnant as some would like to purport.

THE NATURE AND STRUCTURE OF PRE-COLONIAL AFRICAN ECONOMY AND ITS MAJOR OBSTACLES EXAMINED

◆ ◆ ◆

The structure of the economy in pre-colonial period was chiefly in agricultural, non-agricultural productions, exchange and marketing of commodities, and it also consisted of services as stated earlier, all this would in turn be analysed.

AGRICULTURE

◆ ◆ ◆

Undoubtedly, the first rule of life is survival. And pertinent to human survival is the resultant produce from agriculture among others. This was perhaps Ogunremi's conception when he avers;

"All over the world agriculture assured supplies of food, stimulates a high degree of urbanization and specialization and encourages an increase in population."[9]

Generally speaking, in pre-colonial West Africa, practice of agriculture was pertinent for survival. It was basically based on "subsistence" farming, i.e., agriculture. More than anything else, the factor that sustained agricultural practices was the initiative and innovations of the farmer. Although unlettered, the traditional African farmer (with indigenous wisdom) had observed the changing seasons over the years and from his investigations, he could reasonably presume the pouring of the rains and the coming of sunshine. He thus determined the start and the end of planting seasons and harvested the fruit of his labour when it was time to do so. Agricultural production relied totally on availability of suitable land and labour.[10] with this in mind, the perceived obstacles to the development of agriculture as evident –in its factors of production (land, labour, capital and entrepreneur) - through the pre-colonial period would constitute a reasonable discourse to which I now turn. It also need to be stated as well, that, for the ease of analysis and its interactive proximity, land and labour would be discussed together, with capital and entrepreneur following the same trend.

Land and Labour

Of all factors of production, land was the only one that seemed to be in abundance. It was unimaginable that a prospective farmer would have any difficulty obtaining land for his use.[11]One thing to note is the land-labour ratio. The land was vast but the people were few. One explanation for this was the Trans-Saharan slave trade, and on a much greater scale, the Trans-Atlantic slave trade.[12] Slavery lasted for well diff over 500 years in West Africa and for nearly 1500 years in East Africa.[13] first, the Slave Trade helped to destroy the growth of population in Africa. Although this loss was spread over more than three centuries, at the peak of the trade in the 18th century, Africa lost about 100,000 men and women every year. It is important to remember that these were men and women in their prime, aged between 20 and 40.[14] thereby evacuating the prime movers of African economy during the period of our discourse. And as expected, when a people loses its productive workforce especially on a large scale economic hardship inevitably results. It was perhaps in expression of this agonizing outpour that a popular Asante saying evolved;

"I call on gold;

Gold was mute;

I call on cloth;

Cloth was mute.

It is Man that matters" [15]

Considering the wisdom behind this saying, it appears that no riches (as gold and cloth was the standard measurement of value then) are as valuable as human being despite its (riches) pertinence to our sustenance. This saying perfectly fits into the supposed defining role of labour in the pre-colonial African economy.

The older people and children that were left for the most part were more dependents than bread winners. Just as this situation imposed serious limitations on labour supply it also adversely affected the growth of markets since those shipped away would have been both producers and consumers. The loss would have been total if some liberated slaves had not returned towards the middle of the 19th century to enrich the socio-economic activities in places like Abeokuta and Lagos.[16] The liberated slaves did not however, return to all those areas that had lost them.[17] It follows from the above that these ex-slaves though returned to Africa but were faced with the problems of integration into this new abode and as such could not rapidly effect any meaningful socio-economic change.

The labour insufficiency problems would have been a bit minimized were it not for the diversion of energies of African to incessant wars. Lucan for example writes about how war ravaged old Ghana's economy; for many years, the kingdom's wealth and power had caused envy among sanhaja Berbers. They had joined together under and under their leader Tilutane, they attacked the provinces in the north of the kingdom.[18] it is instructive to note that this marked the beginning of war series between the berbers and old Ghana which eventually led to her eco-political collapse.

Rodney also calls our attention to this important point as he writes about Yoruba land; early in the 19th century, Oyo and Yorubaland in general began to export captives in considerable numbers. They were obtained partly by military campaigns outside Yorubaland but also through local slave procuring. Local slave procuring involved kidnapping, armed raids, uncertainty and disunity. The famous Yoruba ancestral home of Ife was also despoiled and its citizens turned into refugees, because of quarrels among the Yoruba over kidnapping for sale into slavery.[19] Economic development (as tied to working of the land) becomes hard during this period under the impulse of such uncertain and insecure environment.

Another explanation for the above contention is that, labuor shortage was probably a reflection of the prevalent low life expectancy as usually caused by poor healthcare and high infant mortality rate as explained by peoples' major interest in prolonged human procreation due to the uncertainty by parents as to whether their children would survive them or not.[20]

These scenarios shown above seemed truly stifling to the pre-colonial African economic neuron, but the Africans mitigated it in their own way, as Oyemakinde observed; it must have been both fashionable and desirable to keep large families to increase the chances for a fair number beating death to it until a ripe age would be attained. That seemed to be their solution to the problem of labour shortage which featured prominently in traditional West African economy and even till now.[21] .

Capital and Entrepreneur

Unlike labour which was badly needed although it was in short supply, capital was also scarce but not as critical a need. While it was true that the farmer had to keep some seed for future planting instead of selling or consuming everything, and it was also true that the craftmen and traders had to set aside some wealth for the creation of further wealth, the states of economic production in pore-colonial West Africa was hardly capitalized. The processes were invariably somewhat rudimentary and the cost simple and cheap for the most part.[22]it is pertinent to also note that capital was not only sought from personal saving as contended above but also from friends, family, and community purse.[23]

There is no doubt that there were capital investment which enabled other factors of production to function. There were credit institutions which gave out credits to producers to obtain some of their tools. One of such credit institutions known in Yorubaland of modern Nigeria was *Esusu* - a form of credit association. It was often organized by friends, age groups, and kinsmen. There was the regulation as to how much each person should contribute and at what interest should the contributions be made. At fixed period, a subscriber will collect what all had contributed and it was everyone's turn to collect his share. A general criticism has however been levied against the system, it is found that the proceeds were often than not deployed to social purposes as funerals and marriages. It is also likely that some subscribers spent part of their shares in procuring tools and raw materials for their production.[24] It follows therefore that as organized as the pre-colonial capital system was it was still bedeviled by certain pitfalls.

NON-AGRICULTURAL PRODUCTIONS

◆ ◆ ◆

No doubt Agriculture dominated African pre-colonial economy. But aside this all important venture, there were others which are in no way inferior to, but complementary to it. These includes; gathering, hunting, fishing, pastoralism, mineral working, manufacturing, and craftsmanship.[25] these, like agriculture were also not without some obstacles, an analysis of which engages my attention next.

Gathering and Hunting

This is not only prominent in pre-colonial African economy but also seems to pre-date agriculture and in fact the first port of call for the survival of early Africans. This position was favoured by several scholars, prominent amongst whom was Margaret Sharman[26] as she writes about the Stone Age Africa; "Let us imagine we can go back about 50,000 years in time, and meet the men who lived in Africa towards the end of the 'Old Stone Age'. They are short but very strong, and they are wearing loin clothes made of animal skins. One man is breaking off a stone by hitting it with another stone. He is making a hand-axe. He can kill small animals with his hand-axe, and he can take off the animals' skin with the sharp point. The man's wife cooks the meat by holding it on a stick over fire. From the bushes children collect berries, which they sweeten with honey. This people lives in the open, or in rock shelters, and the man spend their days hunting, and trapping wild animals. They hunt with wooden spears. Thousand of years later, men learned how to live in groups. They sowed seed and planted crops. They made cooking pots of clay, and cloth from the bark of trees. They took over land from the hunting people". Indeed, gathering and hunting are regarded as economic activities mainly because at a stage of development some people subsisted on them, but with time they became only supplementary to agriculture. Hunting tools such as arrows, clubs and other weapons were used to kill animals. Apart from providing protein as food and animal skin as clothes, hunters were known to be path creators and settlement founders. Many of such paths later made roads and their settlements developed into villages and towns. Besides, hunters served as guardsmen in protecting people from attacks of dangerous animals. Thus, they provided security without which economic activities could not go on.[27]

A very important aspect of the economic importance of a hunter was in killing elephants whose tusks were ivory. Exportation of ivory certainly preceded the notorious exportation of human beings across the Atlantic. Writing in the early 16th century, Pereira[28] noted that he and his party bought elephants' tusks in Benin. He also referred to the abundance of ivory in Igboland.

Fishing and Pastoralism

Like hunting, fishing could be a main occupation or a supplementary activity to farming. Also like hunting, it provided an important source of animal protein. In all cases, fishermen used more or less the same methods in catching fishes. Nets, traps of various kinds and sizes, spears, harpoons and poisons were used. All these instruments of catching fishes provided additional economic activities, usually for the fishermen themselves. But canoes which were essential capital for fishing were built by canoe-builders such as the Ijo on the Niger Delta and the Kedeon in Niger. Therefore canoe building itself became a profession subsisting majorly fishing occupation and transportation of people, farm produce and goods. Smoking and selling of fish and its distribution were yet other economic activities connected with fishing. An interesting feature of fishing was in connection with migrations. There were *itinerant fishermen* such as the Hausa and Nupe who obtained temporary fishing rights from local heads for payment in fish. Pastoralism is yet another type of non-agricultural occupation in pre-colonial West Africa. Although both hunting and pastoralism are related in the sense that both dealt with lower animals, pastoralism was, indeed more closely related to farming. Owning to the infestation of the forest areas by the tsetse flies and problems of available large grazing land, pastoralism was confined to the savannah region of West Africa. Among the great pastoralists were the Fulanis. Perhaps, their greatest economic importance lay in the production of cattle on which the forest dwellers relied on for their beef. In the same manner, the leather workers in Hausaland relied heavily on their livestock.

Mineral Working(Mining) and Manufacturing
     It can be strongly suggested that of all mineral works that took place in pre-colonial
West Africa and, indeed Africa, as Ogunremi calls attention towards. Iron working was the most important to the overall economy of the region. There was a close link between iron working, agriculture and political power. With iron smelting, iron tools gradually replaced wooden and stone implements for cultivation, carving and mining. There is no doubt that iron technology revolutionized production whenever it exist Iron metallurgy not only brought economic revolution, it also put political power into the hands of those who know and used it over those who did not. Iron war weapons (technology) such as iron pointed spears were produced. Farmers, warriors and craftsmen depended

on the smiths (iron/blacksmiths) for their swords, scissors, hoes, cutlasses, hammers, knives, spear heads, arrow heads and axes. They sometimes requested smiths to make certain implements they needed.[30]

It is important to note that there was also special category of smiths known as the migrant blacksmiths who moved about to areas where iron-ore was plentiful. For example, smiths from Akwa, the old capital of Zamfara, used to travel to Tureta; near Sokoto, spending two or three months there and returning home with their donkeys loaded with smelted iron before the raining season when there was high demand for agricultural tools. Serious historical study had shown that the Nok area, a village, in central Nigeria, north-east of the confluence of the Niger and the Benue rivers and south-west of the Jos Plateau were known for iron work. Salt like iron was also of crucial importance in every-

day life of the peoples of Nigeria. In the 18th century the main southern terminus of Salt Trade was Katsina and later on, Kano. The other two types of minerals that were very important are copper and tin. Ile-Ife and Benin were reputed for bronze casts. Therefore it is apparent that the technology to produce bronze was known and available to the people. To make bronze there must be a combination of copper and tin. Tin deposit was even more restricted and its smelting highly localized. Extant literature confirmed that tin smelting was done around north of Jos, at

Linmein Dolma[31]

Craftsmanship

It is certainly difficult if not impossible to discuss fully the multifarious works of art and
crafts which pre-colonial Africans engaged in, as Ogunremi calls our attention to, in the pre-colonial era. Among the most conspicuous ones are cloth weaving, pottery, jewellery and leather working. Textile production involved cotton growing, spinning, weaving, sewing, dyeing, and embroidery; although the last two were optional. Cultivation of cotton and dyeing leaves were part

and parcel of farming. Perhaps, Kano was the most important centre of cloth, weaving, dyeing and distribution up to the 19th century. Kano cloth was such of a high quality that there was demand for it as far away as Morocco. Cloth manufacturing was also common in Igbo land Nupeland, in Yorubaland and in Benin. The use of woven cloth in Yorubaland is of considerable antiquity. This is indicated by the terracotta figures in Ife which have been dated to the 12th century.[32] It is also known that the Ijebus were not only among the earliest Yoruba cloth weavers but were also great exporters of cloth. In the 17th century, European merchants carried Ijebu cloths to Benin, the Gold Coast, Gabon, and Angola and by the 18th century, Ijebu cloths were being exported to Brazil. Because Ijebu cloths were relatively cheap and durable, they were sought for from far and wide.[33]

The most notable centres for casting masks, heads and statutes from copper, bronze and brass were Igbo-Ukwu, Ife and Benin. Excavation at Igbo-Ukwu, which had been radio-carbon dated to the 9th century, showed a considerable amount of beads and some glasses. Both Ife terracotta and the Nok sculptures portrayed lovely jewellery and ornament. Bead production was another indigenous industry and the Nupe were and still are the most popular producers in Nigeria. Among other craft industries that existed in pre-colonial Nigeria were calabash making, basketry, leather work, woodwork and rope and mat making.[34]

Leather work relied solely on animal skins. After tanning, leathers were used to manufacture buckets, mallets, bags, cushions, clothing, footwear, tents, furniture and arrow quivers. In some cases it was a substitute for basket, pot, woven cloths, calabash or woodwork. Although, the Nupes, Yorubas and some others engaged in leather works, the Hausas of Kano, Gobir and the Kanuris of Borno were noted for excellent leather works. Gobir, produced not just for local consumption but also for export. Gobir's sandals reached Timbuktu in the 16th century. The sandals were carried to North Africa and probably to Europe. Katsina was, eminently known for excellent leather. Borno too, produced excellent leather, part of which it exported in addition to slaves to North Africa in exchange for horses in particular.[35] This had flourished even before the reign of the popular Mai Idris Aloma. Woodwork involved making vessels, dishes, stools, mortals and pestles, trays, bowls, spoons, bottles, jars and lids, combs, sandals, musical instruments and beds, doors and windows and so on for home use; axe, and hoe handles, hoes and spades for agricultural practices; weapons for warfare, canoes for fishing and transportation and idols and statutes for religion. The canoes made by the Kede in Nupeland and the Ijo in the Niger Delta were renowned.[36]

EXCHANGE AND MARKETING OF COMMODITIES

◆ ◆ ◆

One reason why people in one part of the world establish links with people in other parts of the world is trade.[37]

The export of captives did not stimulate the growth of internal trade in West Africa; it retarded it. The growth of interregional trade and specialization that had been advancing in the centuries preceding the mid-seventeenth — driven by population growth and inter-continental trade — was terminated. The trade in locally produced cotton cloths between the Benin kingdom and its northeastern neighbors (northeastern Yoruba and Nupe) and between Benin and the Gold Coast, which was advancing to proto-industrial production of cotton cloth, was cut off by the direct exchange of captives for imported European and Asian textiles on the Gold Coast. Similar developments occurred in southeastern Nigeria.[38]

The inter-regional trade and specialization, in which the densely populated northern Igbo produced and traded manufactures with the communities on the Atlantic coast and in the river valleys, was replaced with violent procurement of captives from the densely populated northern Igbo and taken to the middle-men traders on the coast without market exchange, in the first instance. The direct exchange of these captives for manufactures brought by the European traders created enclave economies on the coast and the immediate hinterland, as it did on the Gold Coast and elsewhere in the coastal regions of West Africa. Much of what scholars thought was booming trade in West Africa, stimulated by the trade in captives, was largely limited to these enclaves, while the much larger victim areas in the interior lost much of their stimulating inter-regional and local trade, as violence raged.[39] The result of which was a slower pace of economic development.

All this reinforced the adverse effects of the absolute population decline and the decline of inter-continental trade, the two main drivers of the commercializing process in the centuries prior to the mid-seventeenth. This is what is reflected by the stagnant agricultural prices and the decline of demand for local exchange currencies. This is also the reason why Curtin found lack of progress in agricultural technology in Senegambia in the two hundred years preceding 1850, after the changes in the earlier two hundred years. It is, thus, no surprise that the process of agricultural commercialization stalled in the two hundred years period, 1650-1850, resulting in the overwhelming dominance of subsistence agriculture on the eve of European colonial rule in West Africa.[40]

Added to these were the attendant problems of currency and legal tender. Aghalino[41] calls our attention to the fact that trade was a noticeable feature of pre-colonial West African economy. Trade involved multilateral relations and most goods were not readily interchange-able and money played a function of a medium of exchange it must be said however, that when the economy of West Africa was still in its embryonic stage, in the absence of money, exchange was essentially done by barter system; with its attendant problem of double coincident of wants. But as time wore on, prices were assessed through standard currencies which received general acceptance as means of exchange. The currencies include; brass rods, manila, copper wires, cowries, iron rods, cloth and salt. Where guns were accepted as a medium of exchange was in the Niger Delta.[42] While it may be argued that these currencies served relatively, its intended purpose, they are not without some pitfalls.

The cowry, as a trade currency in pre-colonial period, has been subjected to a lot of criticism. It was said to be inadequate for market transaction according to Robbinson, it is claimed that it lacked the three major features of money; namely:- intrinsic value, scarcity and portability.[43] It is also alleged that as there was no government control of its supply, its value fluctuated sometimes violently and in most cases, intermittently. But this problem is not peculiar to the cowry as a currency. Like all forms of currencies, its value sometimes appreciated or depreciated. But, perhaps, it major weakness as a trading currency was that its was very cumbersome to earn' in large quantities.[44] But despite this problems, the cowry performed the function of money. The cowry lacked a convenient unit of high denomination. This, undoubtedly, was a major constraint when a large sum of money was needed in a trading transaction. For example, one bag of cowry weighed about a hundred pounds, and this posed considerable transportation problems. Brass rods, copper wires and Manilla were bedeviled by a number of problems. For example, the transportation of a large quantity of the manilla required special arrangement. Besides, it has been argued that the need for transporting large quantities of the manilla and the brass, rods encouraged slavery and the slave trade. It has been alleged that it created the need for porters to carry these currencies to the market. Just like the cowry, the brass rod, the copper wire and the manilla, being of low unit value, were also difficult to count.[45]

The manilla, brass rods and the cooper wires were definitely cumbersome and could not have been carried about conveniently by one person. However, thirty shillings worth of manilla or brass rod was a lot of money, and so very few people could have had the need to carry such money on a regular basis.[46] But, three hundred and sixty British copper pennies, or a hundred and twenty three penny pieces may have been less cumbersome to carry than their equivalence in manilla or brass rods; yet they were not in any way more convenient to count and carry about. It follows, therefore, that these British coins would also have presented the same counting and transportation problems posed by the brass rods and the manilla. In fact, Aghalino[47] argued for example that, when the British currency became widespread in Nigeria, market women normally carried their coins in a special cloth purse designed for the purpose.

Other forms of commodity currencies were also available in pre-colonial Nigeria. For example, salt and cloth money were widely used as legal tenders. Cloth money was found in many parts of Nigeria, but was dominant only in areas where cowries had failed to penetrate deeply. It was widely used as currency in Kanem-Borno and was referred to as *dandi.*^ The Bura-speaking peoples of Biu, whose most important export commodity was cotton, also used it as currency. The same thing was applicable to the Tiv who used undyed cloth made of strips sewn together, called *Tugudu* or *Ikudu* as currency.[48]

In what is modern day Nigeria, salt was used predominantly as currency in the Niger Delta area and in most parts of Igboland. Salt, molded into small cones, was a currency at Uburu. The people of Bonny exchanged for yams from the people of the hinterland. It is possible that the people in the Benue area may have once used salt as currency because they had important brine springs in places like Keana and Ankei. The great disadvantage of the salt currency was that, if beaten by rain, it dissolved into a valueless solution.[49]

CONCLUSION

◆ ◆ ◆

The starting-point of the analysis developed in the rest of this paper is a brief conceptualization of development- a copious regulation of internal and external situations- as seen in the light of pre-colonial African economy and its attendant inhibiting forces. Supported with the observation that, in Africa, as in most though not all of Sub-Saharan Africa as whole during the same and earlier centuries, land was abundant in relation to labour, in the economic sense that the availability of unskilled labour was a constraint on the expansion of output, but the availability of cultivable land was not. several forces were responsible for this, among which is low life expectancy, high death rates, "inadequate" medical attention and of course the "Great" Slave Trade and Its attendant diversion of Africans' productive energies towards incessant wars and slave raids coupled with a blow on craft. And as a matter of fact, pastoralism was neglected and nearly dragged to a finishing point while manufacturing process were completely annihilated leading thus to alarmingly underdevelopment.[50]

This was at a time when African economy is fast becoming a regional force as seen through the development of intra and inter-regional marketing and exchange system for their surplus.[51] this is again not only truncated by the attendant problems of double coincident of wants (as in the case of dumb trade) and later currency difficulties but also inadequate means of communication and transportation. Onwuibiko[52] puts it thus; "there were no good roads or railways, no large boats on the rivers, and no portable or convenient currency. All these disabilities hampered the development of large scale internal trade until later part of the 19th century and early 20th century when European colonial government began to develop communications and transportation and introduce convenient currencies". This position was presumably informed by a comparism of the European and African economies and civilization. There is no denying the fact that this claim holds some element of truth, but, given the fact that African economy served the Africans before an advent of the European model, suffices evidence that African economy could have as well developed to such "standards". By this, pre-colonial economy of Africa may be argued to have been relatively developed save the fundamental obstacles discussed thus far.

NOTES

◆ ◆ ◆

1. Toyin Falola, *The power of African Cultures,* New York: University of Rochester Press, 2009, 71.
2. S. M. Johnson, *The Nature and Structure of the Pre-colonial Economy of Nigeria,* www.smbafrica.org, 02-04-2016, 03:06pm.
3. O. Awolowo, *The Problems of Africa,* London: Macmillan Educational Ltd., 1977, 20.
4. Volunteers and Development Workers in Global Solidarity, *Annual Reports,* www.comhalamh.org>issuesto-consider, 25-04-2016, 10:12am.
5. W. Rodney, *How Europe Underdeveloped Africa,* Abuja: Panaf Publishing, 2009, 2.
6. This Information was obtained from www.businessdictionary.com ,26-04-2016,03:00am.
7. Ibid.
8. E. W. Nafziger, *The Meaning and Measurement of Economic Development,* www.ebookscambridge.org ,26-04-2016, 10:12am.
9. G.O. ogunremi, *The Structure of Pre-colonial Economy,* in G.O. Ogunremi and E. K. faluyi (eds.), "Economic History of West Africa Since 1750", Ibadan: Rex Charles Publications, 1996, 37.
10. S. M. Johnson, op.cit.
11. Wale Oyemakinde, *The Structure of West African Economy,* in G.O. Ogunremi and E. K. Faluyi (eds.), "Economic History of West Africa Since 1750",.. 3.

12. S. M. Johnson, op.cit.

13. F. k. Buah, *Europe and west Africa,* London: Macmillan Educational Limited, 1967, 65.

14. Ibid. 67.

15. Ibid. 117.

16. Studied in J.F. Ade Ajayi, *Christian Mission in Nigeria,1941-1994,* London: Evans Brothers Ltd., 1965.

17. Wale Oyemakinde, *The Structure of West African Economy,* in G.O. Ogunremi and E. K. Faluyi (eds.), 5.

18. T. A. Lucan, *Visual History of West Africa*, London: Evans Brothers Ltd., 1971, 6.

19. See W. Rodney, *How Europe Underdeveloped Africa,* 136.

20. His discussions on labour recruitment in pre-colonial Africa in G.O. Ogunremi and E. K. Faluyi (eds.), 2.

21. Ibid.

22. Ibid.3.

23. O.M. Ehinmore, M.A Class discussion on *Indigenous Modes of Production in Pre-colonial Africa*, at his office, 24-03-16.

24. G. O. Ogunremi, *The Structure of Pre-colonial Economy,* in G.O. Ogunremi and E. K. Faluyi,(eds.)....15.

25. G.O. Ogunremi, *Traditional Factors of Production in the Pre-colonial Economy* ...37.

26. This is based on discussions in G.O. Ogunremi and E. K. faluyi, (eds), as especially evident in chapters 1-3.

27. Margaret Sharman, *Africa Through the Ages,*London: Evans Brothers Ltd, 1964, 7.

28. Ibid. 1.

29. D.C. Pereira, *Esmeraldo De Situ Orbio*, London: Hakbyt Society, 1937, 127.

30. G.O. Ogunremi, *The Structure of Pre-colonial Economy...,* 21.

31. Ibid. 21-22.

32. Thurstan Shaw, *The pre-history of West Africa,* in J.F. Ade Ajayi and Michael Crowder,(eds.), "History of West Africa", London: Longman,1971, 69.

33. G.O. Ogunremi, *The Structure of Pre-colonial Economy…* 24-25.
34. S. M. Johnson, *The Nature and Structure of the Pre-colonial Economy of Nigeria,* op.cit.
35. Ibid.
36. Ibid.
37. T.A Lucan, *A visual History of West Africa,* London: Evans Brothers Limited, 1974, 1.
38. W. Rodney, *How Europe Underdeveloped Africa,* Abuja… 264.
39. Ibid.
40. Ibid.625.
41. S.O. Aghalino, *Trade and Currencies in Pre-Colonial Nigeria,* in O.N. Njoku (ed.) "Pre-Colonial Economic History of Nigeria", Benin: Ethiope Publishing Corporation, 2002, 86.
42. Ibid.86.
43. C.H. Robinson, *Hausaland or 1500 Miles Through Central sudan,* London: n.p., 155.
44. G.O. Ogunremi, *Counting the Camels: The Economics of Transportation in Pre-Industrial Nigeria,* London: NOK,1982, 43.
45. Ibid.
46. G.I. Jones, *Native and Trade Currencies in Southern Nigeria During the Eighteenth and and Nineteenth Centuries,* in "Africa" Vol.28, No.1, 1958, 43.
47. See Aghalino, *Trade and Currencies in Pre-Colonial Nigeria…87.*
48. C.H. Robinson, *Hausaland or 1500 Miles Through Central sudan,* 156.
49. Ibid.
50. Gareth Austin, *Markets With, Without and Inspite States: West Africa in the Pre-colonial Nineteenth Century,* London: London school of Economics, 2014, 15.
51. S.O. Aghalino, *Trade and Currencies in Pre-Colonial Nigeria…90.*

52. K.B.C. Onwubiko, *School Certificate History of West Africa, 1800-Present Day,* Onitsha: Africana-Fep Publishers, 1973, 4.

THANK YOU